THE WRITER'S WORKBOOK

A Full and Friendly Guide to Boosting Your Book's Sales

By *Sensible Solutions'*
Judith Appelbaum & Florence Janovic

PUSHCART

To: Authors of Upcoming Books

First of all, Congratulations! Getting a publisher for your book is a triumph. Second of all, Watch out. No matter how prestigious or enthusiastic your publisher is, your book probably won't be treated the way it should be.

It's not that publishers don't want to support their books, or that they don't know how to generate sales; it's just that they don't have enough staff and money to give each book the attention it needs and deserves. As a result, most general-interest titles fizzle out fast.

That's why smart authors get involved, and why this Workbook was written. It offers practical, low-cost ways for writers to give their books their shot at success, ways that have worked for Sensible Solutions clients over the years.

We know that informed, intelligent writers can do what publishing staffers would do if they had the resources. And we've designed this Workbook to share our expertise. It will guide you through the major phases of the publishing process, providing step-by-step advice on how to better your book's fate.

In each phase, it's important to play your part in a style that's right for you and for the publishing professionals you encounter. Some houses are more enthusiastic about author involvement than others, and some people will welcome your activism while others will be wary. So if one approach doesn't seem to evoke the response you'd like, simply pull back and try another.

When you blend your knowledge with determination and courtesy, you should be able to guide your book through the publishing house and out to readers both gracefully and effectively.

– Judith Appelbaum
– Florence Janovic

Dedicated to all the writers,
past, present and still unproven,
who have given us and will give us
countless hours of immeasurable pleasure.

Contents

Making the Book   1

Marketing the Book   13

Making the Book ———

Shaping your manuscript to be the best book it can be involves editors, copyeditors, designers and production people. You have a role to play with each, but it's a much bigger role with some than with others.

Most editors and copyeditors will welcome, even actively seek, your considered opinions on changes in the text. If disagreements arise that can't be easily resolved, they're likely to let you have the last word.

By contrast, designers and production people won't expect to get your views and may feel – often correctly – that they're better equipped than you are to make wise choices about type, layout, margins, paper, binding, color and so forth.

The four sections that follow present specific ways to help ensure that your book reads well and looks good.

Editorial Affairs

The editorial department is responsible for acquiring manuscripts and improving them. In addition, individual editors are supposed to follow acquired manuscripts through all the stages of the publishing process – copyediting, production, sales and so on – making suggestions, offering criticism and facilitating progress. Your editor is your book's representative in the house.

Some editors will do their job more energetically and effectively than others.

All editors will act more energetically and effectively for some books than for others.

Tactics

❑ To get a sense of how the publisher perceives your work, find out whether your editor has a record of acquiring successful books; what books on the editor's current calendar are competing with yours for attention; what other books the house will be publishing at about the same time it publishes yours (they'll be your competition in the struggle for attention from the sales force); what books comparable to yours the publisher has done previously, and what sorts of sales histories they had.

❑ You may want to foster some expectations and counter others. Either way, it pays to know what the publisher foresees.

❑ To communicate with various people at the house, work through your editor, but establish direct relationships with others quickly, asking your editor to put you in touch with each person who will be handling your book at any point.

❑ Once you've set up direct lines of communication with people in a variety of departments, keep your editor informed by mail or phone of any significant discussions you will have and have had with them.

❑ Sometimes the editor who acquires a manuscript will turn it over to someone else for line editing – i.e., reorganization, rewording, expansion, cutting and other substantive changes.

❑ Find out who's going to line edit your book and, if it's a new player, ask to be introduced. Communicate directly with the line editor about the manuscript itself.

❑ Immediately after your manuscript is accepted, ask your editor to return it to you briefly so you can go over it once more, noting every point that matters to you that might be affected by line editing and/or copyediting. When you send the ms. back, attach a covering letter flagging these points.

"Here's the manuscript, complete with marginal notes about my favorite passages, stylistic preferences, and such like. Naturally, I'd be happy to discuss differences of opinion (if they exist)."

❏ Check your copy of your book's production schedule to confirm that it provides for preparation of relevant supplementary sections, like an index or a glossary.

❏ Write your editor to confirm that you will have a chance to see the edited ms. of your book, the copyedited ms., the title, the layout, the illustrations (if there are any) and the captions, the cover or jacket design and flap copy and the catalogue copy *before they go into production.* As an extra precaution, a visit to the office near deadline times should help guarantee that nothing gets by without your seeing it first.

❏ Find out who the cover or jacket artist will be and when the artist will submit sketches. Write a note to your editor saying when you expect to have blurbs for the cover and conveying any suggestions you may have about artwork, relative importance of words in your title, flap and backcover copy, etc. (See "Design.")

❏ Check the deadline for catalogue copy and estimates of how much space your book is going to get. Assess style and content in the current catalogue; then draft copy for your book accordingly and present it to your editor in good time.

❏ Respond to substantive editing thoughtfully and constructively.

Example_____

"I am very grateful, of course, for the time and trouble you've taken with the manuscript. In a few spots, I've asked that my original wording be restored (I do see your point about Frank's diction but I think that's just the kind of affectation he would be guilty of in such a situation) and I don't think the reorganization of Chapter IV that you suggest will work, but I have tried to rewrite that chapter in order to solve at least some of the problems you were tackling with your plan. I'll call you toward the middle of next week to see whether there's still anything we need to come to terms on or whether the manuscript as it now stands is as fine with you as it is with me."

❏ Check back as pub date nears to see if first-printing figures have been adjusted. The best way to get this information – and answers to most other sensitive questions – is to develop a solid, honest relationship that allows your editor to feel free to tell you the truth, without worrying about destroying your ego or arousing your temper. Say that you're ready to deal with the facts, that ignorance is not bliss and that you're a grown-up who can handle reality.

❑ Keep sending morsels of evidence that relate to the size of the market for your book, and to enthusiasm among prospective readers.

Example _____

"I stopped in at the biggest bookstore here the other day and had a long talk with the owner/manager, who declared that he's done beautifully with books about parenting and that he's always hungry for new parenting titles. When I told him we had one coming up, he was eager for details and said (sincerely, it seemed to me) that he thought all the booksellers in his regional association would be good customers for my book as I described it."

Or:

"As I may have told you, I was one of eighty leaders in the field who met to discuss common problems and strive toward solutions together last week. I mentioned my book, naturally, and the response was extraordinary. Several of my colleagues said at once that such a book was desperately needed, and close to a dozen asked me to get them copies as soon as it was available. They seem to think that the thousands of clients they deal with each year need the book and will want it too."

_____

❑ If your editor leaves the house, don't panic. This is a common publishing snafu. Find out who is now handling your book and meet with the new editor. Then, if you don't sense sufficient enthusiasm or qualifications, ask your original editor who in the house might be better. If the sales manager, the head of the publicity department, the special sales manager or any other key players leave, you should also make it a point to meet with their replacements.

Copyediting _____

The copyediting department is responsible for making the contents of a book factually and grammatically correct, as well as internally consistent and consistent in style. Some houses have a style sheet; others try to discern the author's stylistic preferences (serial comma or no serial comma? theatre or theater?), and aim to follow them.

Copyediting is the step immediately after editing and it usually constitutes the last stage at which textual changes can be made free of cost.

Many copyeditors are freelancers. There's one to a book. You will be actively involved in this stage and it will pay to be clear, quick and cooperative.

If you know of a particular copyeditor you'd like to have work on your manuscript, talk to your editor in good time about the possibility.

Tactics _____

❑ Write a note to the copyeditor to call attention to the marginal notations you made on the ms. and to ask for help with troublesome questions.

Example _____

"I'd be grateful if, in the course of copyediting my book, you'd (1) double-check the references to the bibliography that appear in the text to see if I've included everything I promised; (2) not use any sexist language (and let me know if I used any by mistake), and (3) not use Mr., Ms., Mrs., Miss or any other honorifics except those that function as job titles (e.g., Sen., Dr.). Please call if I can be helpful in any way (555-5555)."

❑ Send a copy of your note to your editor.

❑ Your copyedited ms. is likely to be bristling with queries on the copy itself and on slips of colored paper pasted onto the pages. Don't take this as criticism. A good copyeditor can greatly improve your work. Rather, respond to these as one professional to another.

Example _____

"On the 'the' vs. 'a' thing (1st instance on page 3-A of ms.), I maintain that when writing from within a point of view, what the character can see is already established, whether established in prose or not, the same way that you might notice (establish in your mind) a coffee table upon entering a room long before you mention the table in your conversation (or even put anything on it). Thus 'the' has been used throughout to indicate those things and people already noticed by the p.o.v. prior to mentioning it in narration or dialogue; 'a' is used to indicate those objects and people not previously noted. Since I'm quite a nitpicker on this, I am (at this point — pg. 3-A of ms.) fairly confident I've been consistent. Sorry if this usage is not standard. It is stylistic, but for the substantive reasons I've just indicated."

❑ On minor points, simply write your responses on the flags.

❑ Copyeditors are seldom appreciated. The pay is low and so is their status. Respect their professionalism and express your gratitude.

❑ Common proofreading symbols you may encounter and/or want to use include these:

EXPLANATION	MARGINAL MARK	ERRORS MARKED
Take out letter, letters, or words indicated.	ℒ	He opened the windoѡw.
Insert space.	#	He opened theⱯwindow.
Turn inverted line.	@	(He opened the ⱳopuıɯ.)
Insert letter.	e	He opɅned the window.
Set in lowercase.	ℓc	He Øpened the window.
Wrong font.	wf	He opeɟed the window.
Broken letter. Must replace.	×	He ɤpened the window.
Reset in italic.	ital	He opened the _window_,
Reset in roman.	rom	He opened _the_ window.
Reset in bold face.	bf	He **opened** the window.
Insert period.	⊙	He opened the windowⱯ
Transpose letters or words as indicated.	tr	He(the window opened.)
Let it stand as is. Disregard all marks above dots.	stet	He ~~opened~~ the window.
Insert hyphen.	=/	He made the proofⱯmark.
Equalize spacing.	eq #	HeⱯopened the window.
Move over to point indicated. [if to the left; if to the right]		[He opened the window.
Lower to point indicated.	⊔	He opened the window.⌐
Raise to point indicated.	⌐	⌐He opened the window.⌐
Insert comma.	⋏	Yes he opened the window.
Insert apostrophe.	⋎	He opened the boys window.
Enclose in quotation marks.	⋎⋎ ⋎⋎	HeⱯopenedⱯthe window.
Enclose in parenthesis.	( )	HeⱯJohnⱯopened it.
Enclose in brackets.	[ ]	HeⱯJohnⱯopened it.
Replace with capital letter.	cap	≡he opened the window.
Use small capitals instead of type now used.	sc	He opened the _window_.
Push down space.	⊥	He opened the window.
Draw the word together.	◠	He op ened the window.
Insert inferior figure.	⟨2⟩	Sulphuric Acid is H₂SO₄.
Insert superior figure.	⟨2⟩	2a + b² = cₓ
Used when words left out are to be set from copy.	out, see copy	HeⱯwindow.
The diphthong is to be used.	ae͡	Caesar opened the window.
The ligature of these two letters is to be used.	fi͡	He filed the proof.
Spell out words marked with circle.	spell out	He opened the (2d) window.
Start a new paragraph.	¶	door. He opened the
Should not be a paragraph. Run in.	no ¶	door. ⌐He opened the window.
Query to author. Encircled.	(was?)	The proofⱯread by.
This is the symbol used when a question mark is to be set. NOTE: _A query is encircled._	?	Who opened the windowⱯ
Out of alignment. Straighten.	═	He opened the window.
1-em dash.	⊢em⊣	He opened the windowⱯ
2-em dash.	⊢2/em⊣	He opened the windowⱯ
En dash.	⊢en⊣	He opened the windowⱯ
Indent 1 em.	☐	] He opened the window.
Indent 2 ems.	☐☐	] He opened the window.
Indent 3 ems.	☐☐☐	] He opened the window.

Design ————————————————————————

The design department is responsible for deciding how each book will look. It's the designer's job to devise a physical form for the book (format, typeface and size, chapter heads, etc.) that follows and enhances editorial content and is economical to produce. Designers are often freelancers; as a rule, only one designer works on a book.

You're not likely to be asked about your design preferences, but if you have views you can make them known with discretion.

Tactics ————————————————————————

❑ Familiarize yourself with the basics of design by looking through the books on your own shelves and through *Bookmaking*, by Marshall Lee, second edition (R. R. Bowker); it's available in most libraries.

❑ Bear in mind that the typefaces your publisher will choose among will be those found in a particular typesetter's type book. The samples below give some sense of the range of typographic possibilities.

ITC Bolt Bold®
abcdefghijklmnopqrstuvwxyz
ABCDEFGHIJKLMNOPQRSTUVW
XYZ1234567890 .,;:"&!?$

ITC New Baskerville™ Semi-Bold Italic
abcdefghijklmnopqrstuvwxyz
ABCDEFGHIJKLMNOPQRSTUVWXYZ
1234567890 .,;:"&!?$

Univers® Light Ultra Condensed 49
abcdefghijklmnopqrstuvwxyz
ABCDEFGHIJKLMNOPQRSTUVWXYZ
1234567890 .,;:"&!?$

ITC Avant Garde Gothic® Medium
abcdefghijklmnopqrstuvwxyz
ABCDEFGHIJKLMNOPQRSTUVWXYZ
1234567890 .,;:"&!?$

Franklin Gothic Condensed Italic
abcdefghijklmnopqrstuvwxyz
ABCDEFGHIJKLMNOPQRSTUVWXYZ
1234567890 .,;:"&!?$

Caslon Open Face
abcdefghijklmnopqrstuvwxyz
ABCDEFGHIJKLMNOPQRSTUVW
XYZ1234567890 .,;:"&!?$

Trade Gothic® Bold No. 2
abcdefghijklmnopqrstuvwxyz
ABCDEFGHIJKLMNOPQRSTUVWXYZ
1234567890 .,;:"&!?$

Times Roman®
abcdefghijklmnopqrstuvwxyz
ABCDEFGHIJKLMNOPQRSTUVWXYZ
1234567890 .,;:"&!?$

Helvetica® Thin
abcdefghijklmnopqrstuvwxyz
ABCDEFGHIJKLMNOPQRSTUVWXYZ
1234567890 .,;:"&!?$

Americana Bold
abcdefghijklmnopqrstuvwxyz
ABCDEFGHIJKLMNOPQRSTUVWXYZ
1234567890 .,;:"&!?$

❑ Analyze the relative importance of headings and sections in your text and offer your findings to the designer.

Example

"As you will see, my book is divided into four parts, each of which has a number of chapters. Because each of the parts is presented by a different character, there's a real discontinuity between them, and I hope each one can start on a right-hand page that says only "Part X" in some dramatic type.

The Preface to the book is just something I had to include for political reasons and I'd like it to be set up so the reader would be tempted to skip it. The Afterword, on the other hand, is part of the story the book tells, so I think it should look like the preceding chapters."

❑ If there are books you'd like your book to resemble because they create the same feeling you want yours to create, send them along or send copies of sample pages.

Example

"For what it's worth, the chapter headings in the book I've enclosed seem to me to have a kind of Victorian air about them that would suit my book. I hope something like this will appeal to you, too."

❑ Check the information you have about deadlines for cover or jacket artwork and copy. If you would like any particular artwork included (a photograph of yourself, for example) and/or if you want any particular text to be considered for inclusion (blurbs from celebrities and perhaps copy about the book and about yourself that you've drafted), check to see that your editor has informed the designer and the cover or jacket artist. Then get your materials in on time, keeping your editor apprised.

❑ Find out when you will see sample pages.

❑ You may want to examine the sample pages not only in terms of how they look, but also in terms of how they feel. Check to see whether this is the paper stock that will actually be used in your book and, if it isn't, ask for a sample of that, but bear in mind that your veto power is limited.

Production

The production department sees to it that books are manufactured economically and according to specifications (specs). This is the department that deals directly with the type-setter, the printer and the bindery.

It is the production manager's job to keep each book moving on schedule by coordinating the deadlines that are set for it at its various stages with the deadlines that are set for all the other books the house is processing at the same time.

Tactics

❑ Assuming your editor has agreed to have you see the cover or jacket before it goes into production, let the production manager know that, and request that someone in the department double-check that you have seen it so the house can avoid the extra expenses it would incur if you spotted mistakes after production.

❑ If you have reason to use them, ask (through your editor) for blow-ups of the cover or jacket art for your book that you can display in promoting it. (Later on you might want to request posters composed of quotes from reviews, blurbs and interviews.)

❑ Promptly and carefully read galleys when they arrive, marking essential corrections and changes, and noting, when you can, which changes were necessitated by the typesetter's mistakes (mark these PE — for printer's error — in the margins). PEs are corrected at the typesetter's expense. AAs (author's alterations) are charged to the publisher and — once a sum specified in your contract is reached — to you, so keep them to a bare minimum.

❑ Find out — from your editor or from the production manager if the two of you have established a relationship — how many galleys will be forthcoming and when. Bound galleys are sent to review media that have long lead times and to celebrities who may provide prepublication blurbs. If you think too few bound galleys are going to be produced, write or call your editor and explain how many you think you need, for whom and what makes you believe the expense will prove worthwhile. Then drop the production manager a note to confirm the new order if your editor agrees to put it in. (See "Publicity.")

Although bound galleys are expensive to produce, advance blurbs can be priceless, so it's important to deploy the galleys wisely and do everything you can to make sure you get favorable comments from influential early readers.

❑ Double-check to see when bound books will be available.

❑ If you garner good quotations from reviews, impressive sales and/or book club adoptions after the book is on sale, consider ways these might be used on the cover or jacket in subsequent printings. Discuss options and deadlines with your editor and the production manager.

Marketing the Book

The marketing department devises strategies to get individual books to readers and coordinates the activities of sales, promotion, advertising and publicity people.

Large houses usually direct marketing efforts to "the general reader" through book media, book retailers and book wholesalers. This approach may work well for a title that's positioned as a blockbuster. Encouraged to notice it, people in "the trade" who praise it and stock it can make it take off as planned.

Unfortunately, though, the book trade route spells trouble for non-blockbusters since it implicitly defines them as also-rans.

To get your book its share of the limelight, establish it in its own arena. Concentrate on the book's special-interest audiences, the people who are most likely to be receptive to it and to tell others about it. Once you get word of mouth going in the special "target" markets you've defined, it may ripple out until, eventually, both the trade and the general reader sit up, take notice and enthusiastically plunk down their money for your work.

The pages that follow will help you help your publisher's marketing people reach readers via both special-interest and trade channels.

Publicity

In a small house the publicity department may consist of only one person who is also the advertising department. In a large house, the department will consist of several people, each with a specialty — someone may handle print publicity and reviews while someone else works on radio and TV. No matter how many staff members are involved, the purpose of a publicity department is to get time and space devoted to a house's books without paying directly for that exposure.

Bear in mind that publicity directors must give most books the bare minimum of time and energy, which usually means they send review copies and a release to a relatively small and entirely standard list.

Tactics

❑ The amount of publicity a book will get is ordinarily largely determined by the house's expectations about its sales and by the publicity department's perception of you as a public person.

Therefore, try to arrange a meeting with someone from the department early on to introduce your book's strengths and your special abilities as a speaker or entertainer. Before you bristle, understand that an "entertainer" is what the radio and TV people are looking for; although you may never have considered yourself in those terms, or wanted to, your readiness to do something besides simply talk will make it possible for the publicity department to book you. Can you show how to make an object? Conduct an experiment? Are there film clips that relate to your work? What topics could you and other experts debate before an audience? A list of ideas and approaches that will engage, arouse, or amuse an audience may help the department help you.

Author's Questionnaire
❑ Shortly after your book is accepted, the publicity department will ask you to fill out a detailed author's questionnaire.

Do this as thoroughly and as imaginatively as you can, with as much concrete, specific information as possible. What in your background will help promote this book? What special expertise do you have? Contacts? Previous jobs, experiences?

Blurbs
❑ Compile a list of relevant celebrities (in your field and/or in the world at large) who might praise your book effectively.

Then discuss it with your editor and the publicity people, adding and subtracting from your list according to their suggestions and deciding which of you will approach which celebrities for blurbs (the trade term for endorsements, as opposed to reviews). Then start using the Blurb Writers and Reviewers worksheets.

❑ In order to get blurbs circulating in the publishing house early enough to start ripples of enthusiasm moving, ask for a few even before the book has been set in type (you can send out copies of your edited manuscript). Later, potential blurb writers can get bound galleys, but all blurb solicitations should be timed so that quotes will arrive before cover or jacket copy goes to press. As many as possible should be included on the cover or jacket of your book. (See "Production.")

Reviews
❑ Ask to see the list of review media scheduled to get your book, and suggest additions (preferably with compensating deletions) or substitutions. For instance, you might request that your book go to the lifestyle editors or the business editors or the science editors of major print media rather than to book reviewers if specialists are more likely to be interested in it.

In any event, make sure the review copy list includes all relevant special-interest radio and TV shows and publications and all media in places you have some significant connection with, like areas where you've lived or gone to school. Use the directories listed in Resources and watch *Publishers Weekly* for new periodicals.

❑ If galleys are not ready in time to meet review media deadlines, ask the publicity people to make, bind and send out copies of your manuscript instead.

❑ With your editor and publicity people, compile a list of writers and/or authorities who would be especially receptive to your book and write or call them to see if they'll approach particular publications and ask to review it. The Blurb Writers and Reviewers worksheets will be helpful here too.

Hometown Blitz
❑ Help the publicity people plan a hometown blitz for your book by identifying local bookstores, libraries, organizations (religious, fraternal, social, educational, alumni, recreational, community, etc.) where you might appear to talk about it, as well as by getting up your list of local media and media people. (New Yorkers should think in terms of their neighborhoods — local papers, organizations, schools, religious or social groups.)

Announcements
❑ Arrange for cards announcing publication of your book — and including ordering information — to be sent to friends and colleagues who might order it and thus begin generating word-of-mouth sales.

Parties
❑ Like a *New York Times* ad, publication parties appeal to an author's ego, but unless you can guarantee an impressive press turnout, the money can be better spent elsewhere. Do, however, arrange a party with friends and people from the house if that appeals to you.

The Release
❑ The publicity department usually prepares a press release about each new book for newspaper and magazine editors and reviewers. Consider

drafting it yourself in order to stress angles that reveal the book as timely, important, newsworthy or especially amusing. Ask for samples from the house files if you'd like to follow a model and consider submitting alternative opening paragraphs if your book has more than one sizable, identifiable audience (perhaps, for instance, professionals in its field as well as amateur enthusiasts will be interested in it). If possible, tie your book in with a story that's making news (i.e., give it a "newspeg"). Once the release is ready to go out, add personal handwritten notes to highlight particular angles for particular recipients.

Example

One author wrote a gossip columnist: "I live with my parents in Brooklyn. We are very poor but we are honest and good and gossip-minded." The lines evoked sufficient curiosity to make the columnist scan the book, and variations of this ploy worked successfully with a number of major columnists.

Radio and TV

❑ With particular radio and TV shows in mind, come up with good questions the interviewers might ask you and ideas for theme segments that will make you more than just another author. When you are scheduled to appear on shows, don't count on the interviewers having read your book. Make a list of questions they might ask you and submit it in advance or bring it with you. Try to be anecdotal in your responses.

❑ When you present your ideas and your questions, ask whether the publicity people will try to book you on "phoners," radio shows that interview authors by telephone. These provide wonderful exposure — talking from the comfort of your own home or office, you may get as much as an hour of air time.

❑ Wear comfortable clothes, nothing tight, short or constraining, when you are on the air. Studios (both radio and TV) tend to be hot and airless. For TV, avoid busy prints, solid black or white, and jingling jewelry. Bright colors come across well. Try not to move around a lot or use your hands; it's distracting. Ask the make-up department, if there is one, to touch up your face before a TV appearance. Unless you're told otherwise, ignore the camera and talk to the interviewer.

❑ Carry a clean copy of your book with you when you do a show in a studio, in case the program's copy got lost or taken home. Also, bring written information on how to get the book by mail and via an 800 number, and leave it with the program office and/or the switchboard operator. If your publisher doesn't have a toll-free number that the public can use to place orders, try to make arrangements with a local bookseller or with BOOK CALL (1 800 ALL BOOK).

❑ It's always nice to send a short "thank you" note to the producers and/or hosts of shows you're on.

Tours and Other Travels

❏ If you go on tour, get a list from the sales department or from the *American Book Trade Directory* of the major bookstores in the cities you'll be visiting. Salespeople there should be alerted; write or call the house reps who cover those cities well before your visit to see what steps they plan to take and what bases you will need to cover.

❏ Whenever you plan a personal or business trip, let the publicity people know a couple of months in advance so they'll have time to drum up some interviews. Suggest specific contacts and topics when you can.

Prizes

❏ Have your publisher submit your book for any prizes that are given in your field (see *Literary and Library Prizes*, published by R. R. Bowker).

Directories

❏ Research the directories in your field and write to their editors to ask to be listed (see *Books in Print*).

Results

❏ If your book doesn't seem to be getting reviewed or mentioned anywhere, the trouble may be only that you don't know about coverage. Many houses hire clipping services to monitor periodicals for mention of their books. Some houses forward copies of each clipping to the author, but some don't. Let your editor know that you'd like to receive all clips. If, in fact, your book is getting too little attention or none, go back to your original list of review media and potential reviewers with new information and angles.

❏ As good reviews, lecture bookings, reprintings and other happy events transpire, keep a record and eventually get up a memo and/or a collection of selling quotes to circulate in-house so that the publicity department can think about doing a new release (which you might draft) and the sales department can recall the book to booksellers' attention.

Subsidiary Rights _____

The subsidiary rights department is responsible for selling reprint rights, foreign rights, book club rights and serial (i.e., periodical) rights, including newspaper syndication rights, that aren't reserved by agents. In this area, your ideas and contacts can be very important.

Tactics _____

❑ If your book is a hardcover original and if you've not heard a thing about a paperback sale six months after pub date, ask your editor to check with the sub rights director about the book's status. Has it been sent to reprinters for their consideration? Is your publisher considering bringing out its own paperback edition?

❑ If you have well-founded opinions on the timing of a paperback edition, share them. (Is a major international conference on your subject scheduled for the fall of next year? Will a relevant centennial be celebrated around the time a new edition could be ready? Pub dates might be adjusted to capitalize on such events.) Similarly, if you know which houses often reprint books like yours, pass your knowledge along.

❑ The Book-of-the-Month Club and the Literary Guild may or may not be interested in your book. Unless you have a close connection on their staffs, you should simply abide the outcome there and familiarize yourself with special-interest book clubs.

❑ Look at the book club listings in *Literary Market Place* (See "Resources"); draw up a list of those clubs you think are possible candidates (e.g., the Dance Book Club for a biography of Suzanne Farrell, the Irish-American Book Society for a novel set in Cork); and give the list to the sub rights director as a helpful suggestion.

❑ In the area of serial sales, your activities can do a lot to create excitement for your book. Serial sales involve excerpts from your book sold to magazines and newspapers before and after publication. Periodicals that run excerpts before pub date buy first serial rights and pay more for them than periodicals that run excerpts after pub date, buying second serial rights. Both can be extremely rewarding in terms of publicity generated.

❑ Make a list of publications whose readers figure to be interested in your book. Include not only large national periodicals but also smaller circulation journals and magazines that reach your target audiences. For the latter, look at the *Gale Directory of Publications, Hudson's Newsletter Directory, Standard Periodical Dictionary, The International Directory of Little Magazines and Small Presses,* and *Reader's Guide to Periodical Literature,* as well as at magazines, newspapers and newsletters you receive. (These directories will also be of use in connection with publicity and advertising.)

❑ Go through your manuscript, pulling sections that can stand on their own. Perhaps you will need to add a new lead or bridging material. Maybe some sections can be condensed; or new articles based on your book can be drafted. You may end up with as many as ten or twenty story ideas from or based on your book. Match the stories to the markets in the list you've compiled of relevant periodicals. For each story, have a #1 market and a #2 back-up. Then share your ideas.

Example

"My first choice for the chapter on investing in the stock market would be Lear's *magazine, because it is aimed at affluent subscribers who are likely to be interested in investment strategy. However, if that doesn't work, I would suggest* Men's Life, *aimed at "mainstream" (rather than extreme) middle-aged men who would also welcome the information."*

❑ After discussing your suggestions with the proper sub rights person or your agent, submit query letters to selected periodicals. Decide in each case whether the submission should come right from you or from your agent or the sub rights department, and note plans on the Excerpts and Adaptations worksheet.

❑ If and when a piece is accepted, ask that information about how to get your book be included in the credit line that runs with the piece. For original articles, both those related to your book and those that are not, also ask that the author's bio identify you as the author of ..., from [your publisher].

❑ Newspaper syndicates buy the rights to sell sections of a book to subscribing papers. If your book gets sold to a syndicate, tell the sub rights director about any cities where readers will be especially responsive (if, for example, you've written an exposé of radiation leaks, note where they have occurred). This will make it easier for the syndicate sales force to place your book with selected newspapers. As additional papers buy material from your book, additional modest fees will come in.

❑ If pub date is drawing near and you've heard no news of serial sales, draft a status report letter and ask for follow-up action.

Example

"I have just done some stock-taking and determined that the following projects are stuck in mid-passage. I'd be grateful for anything you can do to get things unstuck. In April we submitted Chapter 5 to Prevention, *but have not heard anything since. In May we sent Chapter 6 to* Family Circle, *at their request, but no response has yet come in. The same week, several chapters (3, 7 and 8) were sent to* Redbook *for consideration. No word. On the other hand, what wonderful news that was about* Family Health *and* The New York Times *syndicate sale! Thank you.'*

Special Sales

Publishers are increasingly interested in selling books to special-interest, target markets, often through nontraditional outlets such as health-food stores, sporting goods stores and other retail operations that aren't bookstores, as well as through catalogues, conferences, conventions, and premium arrangements, among other things.

Some houses now have a special sales department (or director); others parcel special sales efforts out among various departments.

Tactics

❑ Check to see what special sales capabilities the house has and who's in charge. If important markets will be neglected because the house can't deal with them, consider becoming a special sales force for your book yourself.

❑ To get your book into nonbookstore retail outlets, pinpoint the stores whose customers would want it and get up a list. (*Cheap Chic*, a fashion book for women, sold widely and well in clothing stores, for instance; similarly, crafts books often do well in sewing and fabric shops.)

❑ If you will be representing yourself in your special sales effort, consider calling some of the largest and best stores (including chains) of the kind that would work for your book and asking them to recommend salespeople who might be interested in representing the book among their other wares. Meadowbrook Press successfully used this tactic for breaking into the toy-store market with their books about children.

❑ Catalogues provide an excellent way to sell some books. The mail order gift catalogue is big business and books (including self-help books, health books, children's books and humor books) appear among the items offered. Using the directories listed in Resources and the Catalogue Sales worksheets, get up a list of suggestions and send it to the proper person, together with any samples you've collected of gift catalogue copy for books like yours.

❑ Ask the trade sales department for a list of all house catalogues and ask your editor to round up catalogues from other divisions in the publishing house. Mark those catalogues your book should be included in and present your case to the appropriate people.

❑ Anyplace people in your target audience gather is a place you might display and/or sell your book. Look at directories — especially *The Encyclopedia of Associations*, which the library will have — and at conference schedules from relevant associations you belong to or know about. Make up a list of meetings where your book might sell and ask the special sales people to explore the possibility of shipping books and/or order forms to the meetings.

Or do that yourself.

❏ Better yet, see if you can get yourself invited to speak at relevant gatherings. Draft a letter describing yourself and your book and listing the topics on which you can speak. Mention any previous speaking experience and favorable response to it. Ask the publicity department to make a mailing of your speaker's letter to a list of people you select.

❏ When you're invited to speak anywhere, notify the publicity department immediately. Ask if they can arrange TV, radio or print interviews in the city you'll be visiting.

❏ So you'll be able to follow up on the enthusiasm generated by your talk, arrange for books to be on hand when you speak. Sometimes the group will buy copies wholesale and sell them at the cover price; sometimes you'll have to do the buying and selling. In any case, the publisher will probably need at least six weeks notice to ship books.

❏ When you go to speak, bring as many books as you can carry in case the publisher's order does not arrive. Always carry a supply of attractive order forms. (See "Mail Order.")

❏ Contact the sales department so the local rep can make sure area stores are stocked with your book.

❏ When you return from your speaking engagement, send a letter to your editor and copies to other key people in the house describing the enthusiasm with which your talk was received and the number of books sold and any other selling news.

❏ The most lucrative sort of special sale may be the sale of a book as a premium. Books offered as premiums can be prizes in a contest or giveaways to attract new customers or increase purchases of a product. Premium sales generally involve between tens and hundreds of thousands of copies (and dollars). Therefore, although the vast majority of ideas for premium sales don't pan out, possibilities are worth exploring. Start by looking for a connection between your book and a product (e.g., a cookbook for a company dealing with a food featured in it; a book about moving for moving companies). For names and addresses of companies, look through *Thomas Register of American Manufacturers* in your library's reference room.

❏ Even if your book does not seem a natural as a tie-in, a company may want to offer it as a premium. As long as it's a product that can attract new customers to a business, it can be considered as an incentive gift. For example, a bank in New York offered a directory of activities for children as one of a variety of gifts for new accounts.

❏ Books are sometimes used as incentives for joining clubs and organizations. If you've written a career guide for women, for instance, local and national women's business groups might want to buy it in bulk. For tie-ins with organizations, look at *The Encyclopedia of Associations* and *National Trade and Professional Associations of the United States and Canada.*

Mail Order

A number of houses have mail order departments. If the house you're with doesn't, ask your editor whether they ever market through mail order and, if so, under what circumstances and who's in charge. If not, consider launching a modest mail order campaign for your book yourself if you can come up with lists of periodicals whose readers are virtually certain to want to buy copies.

Mail order includes direct mail, which entails sending promotional literature that solicits orders to individual potential buyers through the mail, and space advertising, which involves placing coupon ads in selected periodicals. (See "Advertising" and the section on catalogues in "Special Sales.")

Tactics

❑ Get catalogues of mailing lists (see Resources and the "Mailings Lists" section of *Literary Market Place*). List catalogues are generally free to people who request them on company letterheads, which your publisher can supply.

❑ Devise an angle for each audience you would like to reach and draft an appropriate letter. As a model, use promotional literature you've received and admired or ask the mail order department for copies of successful mailing pieces they have sent.

Remember that potential readers want to know what good your book will do them. Your headline and the copy that follows should make it clear that they'll benefit by reading your book and suffer if they don't. See the Mail Order Worksheet.

❑ Out of the thousands available, check the lists most likely to pull for your book. The following examples appear on a portion of one page from the Dunhill International List Company, Inc., catalogue and hint at the range of groups to which mailing lists provide access.

SIC	SIC Description	Total Compiled Names	SIC	SIC Description	Total Compiled Names	SIC	SIC Description	Total Compiled Names
3321*	Iron Foundries - Gray	2,860	5944I	Lapidaries (Shops)	468	5948*	Luggage & Leather Goods Stores	4,393
3322*	Iron Foundries - Malleable	167	5099U	Lapidary Equipment	230	3161*	Luggage Mfrs.	420
3446G	Iron Ornamental (Wholesale & Mfrs)	2,259	3811B	Lasers (Wholesale & Manuf)	499	5948A	Luggage Repairing	918
7690Q	Ironwork, Service & Repair	3,838	3541A	Lathes (Wholesale & Manuf)	165	5211*	Lumber & Other Building Materials	79,583
4971*	Irrigation System Operations	217	7215A	Laundries - Self Service	13,680	5031*	Lumber, Plywood & Millwork, Whols.	10,815
			7215*	Laundries & Cleaners-Coin Oper	14,076	5211A	Lumber, Plywood & Bldg. Materials	33,191
J			7219*	Laundry & Garment Services, n.e.c.	5,850	5931N	Lumber Used	135
			3582*	Laundry Equipment - Commercial	138	8663Q	Lutheran Churches	16,472
			5087Q	Laundry Equipt Supplies	1,694			
SIC	SIC Description Total Compiled Names		2751B	Law Brief Printers	141	**M**		
3569D	Jacks (Wholesale & Manuf)	527	3524*	Lawn & Garden Equipment Mfrs.	303			
7349A	Janitorial Services	22,969	7394C	Lawn & Garden Equipment-Rental	906	SIC	SIC Description Total Compiled Names	
5087E	Janitors' Supplies, Whols.	7,661	0782D	Lawn Maintenance	14,095	2098*	Macaroni & Spaghetti Mfrs.	374
5411E	Japanese Food, Retail	225	5261C	Lawn Mower Dealers	26,308	5080B	Machine Shop Supplies	115
5611F	Jeans, Retail	1,238	7699E	Lawn Mower Repair/Sharpening Shops	8,498	3599A	Machine Shops - Grinding	34,685
8664N	Jehovah's Witness Churches	3,553	8111B	Lawyers Referral Service	609	3542*	Machine Tool - Metal Forming	922
3915*	Jewelers' Materials & Lapidary Work	293	8111F	Lawyers Service Bureaus	1,378	3545*	Machine Tool Accessories Mfrs.	1,848
5944K	Jewelry - n.e.c.	1,298	7499U	Layouts-Office, Factory, etc	470	3541*	Machine Tools - Metal Cutting	2,642
3911*	Jewelry & Precious Metal Mfrs.	2,128	5051K	Lead (Wholesale)	175	7699T	Machine Tools Repairing	666
5944A	Jewelry Engravers	4,011	3332A	Lead Mills	137	3569*	Machinery - Industrial, n.e.c.	5,444
5094B	Jewelry Findings	373	3952*	Lead Pencils & Art Supplies	196	3599*	Machinery - Nonelectric, n.e.c.	43,747
5094*	Jewelry, Gems & Watches, Whols.	17,506	3332*	Lead Primary Mills	177	5084C	Machinery - New Whls.	2,379
7631C	Jewelry Repair Services	8,631	5051L	Lead Products (Wholesale)	213	5080*	Machinery Equip. Supplies, Whols.	3,732
5944*	Jewelry Stores	46,006	2386*	Leather & Wool - Lined Cloth	131	1796B	Machinery Movers & Erectors	1,434
8664D	Jewish Synagogues	2,859	5199J	Leather & Leather Goods, Whols.	2,380	5093D	Machinery Used	1,32
65B	Fixtures	3	5621D	Leather Clothing, Retail	908			
				Leather Goods Personal	255			

❑ Find out if organizations whose members are likely to want your book will make their mailing lists available (many do, for a modest fee).

❑ Arrange a meeting with the person in charge of direct mail to present your drafts, along with information on prices and sizes of lists you have found.

❑ Draw up a list of the publications where you think small coupon ads could be run to best advantage. Be sure to include special-interest journals and newsletters. (See "Advertising.")

❑ Let your editor know that you would prefer these small coupon ads — which are more likely to sell your book — over large ego-gratifying but cost-ineffective ads in *The New York Times.*

❑ Ask the direct mail department to make up an order form for potential buyers. The form might include a "bill me" option and/or a money-back guarantee along with information on ordering via an 800 number as well as through the mail. It can be as elaborate as a fold-out brochure or as simple as a 5" x 7" card. Try to get the publisher to provide postage-paid return envelopes.

Shown below, both sides of a direct-mail flyer that folds twice to become a self-mailer. Notice the detachable bottom panel — a built-in, postage-paid reply card. The flyer is printed in two colors — black and red — on heavy buff-colored paper.

Bookstore Sales

The sales department's job is to get books into the bookstores. How the sales force perceives your book in large part determines whether the bookstores order it. Not all books are automatically ordered by all stores, and of course quantities ordered vary widely from title to title and store to store. Your job is to make it impossible for the salespeople who call on the booksellers to neglect your book, and, as far as possible, to help the reps focus on its best targets. (See the preceding sections for better target marketing opportunities.)

Tactics

❑ Along with all the other titles on that season's list, your book is presented at a sales conference that the entire sales force attends. The presentation may be made by your editor or the editor-in-chief. Ask your editor when the sales conference covering your book will be held. Often the publisher will give parties for the sales force while they're in town for sales conference. If your publisher is planning any such events, ask if you can attend. Meeting the sales people can only boost your chances that they'll remember and actively sell your book.

❑ Create a package of selling documents to make it easy for the responsible person to present your book persuasively and enthusiastically. The package should go to your editor several weeks before sales conference so that the editor can make copies to pass along to the marketing and sales people. Ideally, a copy of your package will be distributed to every sales person at sales conference.

In the sales kit, you'll want to include:

1) a "handle" for selling your books — a catch phrase or comparative description (e.g., "a novel about the country's shortest pro basketball player...," or, "the most comprehensive guide to camping ever issued"); the sales force needs a handle to use in calls or visits to the stores

2) a list of who will buy your book and why

3) a copy of your Table of Contents if it's especially descriptive of your book, or a paragraph or two summarizing the contents in an inviting fashion

4) a short excerpt from your book that's sure to entertain and whet the reader's appetite for more

5) a bio sheet about you, preferably in narrative form and including a short account of why you wrote the book

6) a list of places where your book is likely to sell well, with reasons in brief, (i.e., your hometown area, the cities where your novel's action takes place, the region where people display the most interest in your subject)

7) a quick, book-by-book analysis of about half a dozen competing titles, with brief explanations of why your book is different from and better than each of them.

❑ Make up a list of bookstores that will be especially good places to sell your book because of location or special-interest focus. See the *American*

Book Trade Directory (available in libraries) for names and addresses. Give your list to the sales manager before sales conference, and develop sales opportunities using the Bookstores Worksheets.

❏ Orders for a specified number of copies of each book are supposed to be secured from booksellers before publication to constitute an "advance sale." Ask what the advance on your book is slated to be, and check as publication date nears to see whether more or fewer copies actually have been advanced. Then try to use surprisingly good sales to spur the sales force on to a more energetic push for your book or, if advance sales are disappointing, consider what you might do to give them a boost. (See below on the no-books-in-the-stores problem.)

❏ Check on sales from time to time. Publishers get frequent computer printouts of the number of copies sold — and returned — on each title. Ask for the figures once a month or so, and if copies in stock seem to be running low, check on reprint schedules.

❏ Confront the no-books-in-the-stores problem with style and sophistication. This is one of the most frustrating situations an author faces. Distribution of books is notoriously crude, and publishers are as bothered by the problem as authors are. Present standard operating procedure depends largely on wholesalers situated throughout the country who warehouse a number of publishers' books and supply them directly to area bookstores. Since booksellers can usually get a full refund for unsold books, there is plenty of opportunity for a book to come and go, even get lost, without a sale being made. Moreover, you can't always trust the information stores give out.

When the no-books-in-the-stores problem strikes you, take the store personnel's explanations ("We ordered it but your publisher hasn't delivered") with a grain of salt and examine these possibilities: The stores never ordered your book; your book took off in a way that your publisher did not anticipate and thus it is out of stock; the bookseller has a credit problem with your publisher; bookstores are not the right place to sell your book.

❏ One way to tackle the problem — once you think you understand it — is by getting your editor involved. If it seems that the sales department does not appreciate your book's potential, consider asking for a meeting with the sales manager to present evidence that your book has a sizable, interested audience; use reviews, articles and blurbs along with data on radio and TV dates, public appearances and other past and future publicity. If bookstores aren't the ideal conduit to your readers, work on special sales (see above).

❏ If the problem is keeping the book in stock, you'll need information on fulfillment snafus, and on how soon a new printing will be available.

Advertising

The advertising department buys space in publications and/or time on radio and TV. Most authors feel their publishers do too little advertising, and too many authors lobby for a big ad in *The New York Times Book Review* without realizing that the expense is enormous and that a single ad is not likely to help sales. An extensive ad campaign in special-interest media, however, can help some books a lot. Later, if your book takes off, advertising in major metropolitan newspapers and/or on mass-market radio and TV programs may make some sense.

Tactics

❑ Analyze what you would consider an extensive ad campaign for your book in the publications whose readers are most likely to want it. (See "Subsidiary Rights.") Get the rates for the appropriate magazines, newsletters, newspapers, radio programs, local TV shows. (Rates can be found in the *Standard Rate and Data Guides;* See Resources.)

❑ Use the Advertising Worksheets to compile information for the advertising department, and present it along with blurbs, information about coordinated events, etc.

Example

"I hope we can run an ad in the June issue because an excerpt from my book will appear in the magazine that month," or, "Please note that a review will run in Saturday's paper; an interview is scheduled for. . . ; local bookstores around Syracuse have placed heavy advance orders," etc.).

❑ When ads run anywhere check to make sure responses will be traceable and ask that mail and phone order instructions be included so that people who read an ad and decide they want your book will have an easy way to get it.

❑ Whenever an excerpt from or an article about you or your book appears, remember to ask that mail and phone order information be included — i.e., get free advertising whenever possible.

Similarly, before an interview on radio or TV ask the host to give mail and phone order information about your book on the air. Type the title, by-line, publisher, price (including postage and handling), mail order name and address and 800 number on a piece of paper to make it easier for the host to oblige and give the same information to the switchboard operator or program office for after-the-show inquiries.

❑ Consider taking out small ads yourself in special-interest publications if your publisher doesn't. Notify your editor of your plans.

❑ Assess the results of ads and see if you can get the advertising department to rerun those that worked.

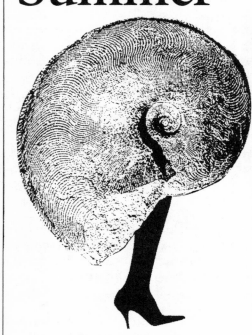

Winner of 1989 Kayden National Translation Award

The Same Sea As Every Summer

By Esther Tusquets
Translated by
Margaret E. W. Jones

Poetic and erotic, *El mismo mar de todos los veranos* was originally published in Spain three years after the death of Franco and in the same year government censorship was abolished. But even in a new era that fostered more liberal attitudes toward divorce, homosexuality, and women's rights, Tusquets' novel was controversial. Its feminine view of sexuality – in particular, its depiction of a lesbian relationship – was unprecedented in Spanish fiction. Now its complex moods and rhythms have been caught in an award-winning English translation. The disillusioned narrator of *The Same Sea As Every Summer* is a middle-aged woman whose unhappy life prompts a journey into the past. A volume in the series, European Women Writers.

$22.95 cloth, $9.95 paper

Also of interest
On Our Own Behalf
Women's Tales from Catalonia
Edited by Kathleen McNerney
$24.95

Nebraska

The University of Nebraska Press · 901 N 17 · Lincoln 68588-0520

This simple, well-designed ad for a University of Nebraska Press title of special interest to women ran in The Women's Review of Books. *The publication often carries ads placed by authors themselves, and produced on their own desktop publishing systems or through the* Review's *production services.*

Library Promotion _____

While almost all publishers have a sales force that calls on (or at least telephones) bookstores, most publishers deal with the huge school, public and institutional library market through a small department headed by a library specialist who issues catalogues and attends conventions. (Librarians tend to select books on the basis of reviews in media they trust — like *Booklist*, *Choice*, *Library Journal* and *School Library Journal* — and to place their orders through jobbers, or wholesalers, that cater specially to library accounts.)

Tactics _____

❑ When your book is accepted, find out what catalogues the house issues for librarians. If your book would fit naturally into one or more, write to bring that fact to the library specialist's attention.

The Mid-Manhattan Library in New York City draws the public to its many free programs with flyers like these. If libraries in your area don't provide similar materials to publicize talks you give, you can easily prepare them yourself.

❏ When your book is published, approach your local librarian(s), introduce yourself and your book and offer to conduct a reading, deliver a lecture, run a workshop or organize and lead some other comrnunity event at the local library or libraries. Draft an announcement of the event for local papers and prepare a flyer for posting and distributing at library checkout desks.

❏ If your book is reviewed favorably by media that librarians respect, ask the library specialist whether a mailing to selected libraries, calling the review(s) to their attention, would be worthwhile.

Example ————————————————————————————————

To promote The Pushcart Prize *to libraries, Bill Henderson mails librarians a postcard with blurbs from sources they respect on the front, and the* Publishers Weekly *review reprinted on the back. Response has been excellent.*

❏ Get a list of upcoming library conferences from your local librarian or the American Library Association and offer to appear at any that seem appropriate because of where they are or what their focus is.

Resources:
A Selective List_____

A wide variety of guides, directories and groups can help you reach the readers who will value your work. Those described here are among the best.

As you'll see, many of them have multiple uses. For instance, you might consult *The Encyclopedia of Associations* to get up a list of newsletters you could advertise in, gatherings you could speak at or people you could contact about premium sales. You might turn to a handbook of nonsexist writing when you were working on serial sales or mail order flyers. You might seek support from fellow members of a writers group at any point in the publishing process.

Because they can come in handy in so many ways, we suggest that you skim through the Resources listings early and often, eyes open for new uses that fit the moment's facts. We've included ordering information for affordable items. If you prefer one-stop shopping, order from Tools of the Trade instead of from individual publishers (3718 Seminary Road, Seminary Post Office, Alexandria, VA 22304-0993; 703-683-4186). Books listed here that are too expensive to own are generally available in libraries.

The ABC's of a Really Good Speech

by Page Emory Moyer
Circle Press
38 The Circle
East Hampton, NY 11937
516-324-5065 or 212-535-4726
1990; $8.95.
If public speaking plays a part in your marketing campaign, this quick and easy guide to pleasing listeners should come in handy.

American Book Trade Directory

R.R. Bowker
245 West 17 Street
New York, NY 10011
800-521-8110
Updated periodically.
An alphabetical listing by state or province and then by city of roughly 20,000 book outlets in the United States and Canada, plus listings of whole-salers and distributors. Valuable for writers who want to identify the stores where their books will sell best. Your bookstore as well as your library should have a copy of the latest edition.

American Library Directory

R.R. Bowker
245 West 17 Street
New York, NY 10011
800-521-8110
Updated periodically.
The listings here, of libraries and library schools in the United States and Canada, make a fine tool for compiling your own library mailing list.

The Authors Guild

330 West 42 Street
29th Floor
New York, NY 10036
212-563-5904.
The guild and its first-rate staff give writers power in working with publishers by providing surveys, newsletters, a sample contract and other valuable forms. The group is active on behalf of authors in Congress and the courts, and its more than 6,000 members include leading literary lights.

Bacon's Publicity Checker

Bacon's
332 South Michigan Avenue
Chicago, IL 60604
Updated periodically.
Look here and in the Gale directory (see below) if you want to compile lists of magazines and newspapers that might welcome a review copy of your book and/or a release about it. You can also buy mailing lists from Bacon's and hire their clipping service.

Bookmaking: The Illustrated Guide to Design/Production/Editing
by Marshall Lee
R.R. Bowker
245 West 17 Street
New York, NY 10011
800-521-8110
Second edition, 1980; $49.95.
A sizable book, with more than 300 illustrations, *Bookmaking* is remarkably complete and well-written. Particularly useful for writers who want to understand what's involved in design and production.

Book Publishing: A Basic Introduction
by John P. Dessauer
Continuum Publishing Company
370 Lexington Avenue
New York, NY 10017
212-532-3650
Third edition, 1990; $24.50.
The essential introductory text for anyone interested in the way publishing works.

Book Publishing Resource Guide
by John Kremer
Ad-Lib Publications
51 North Fifth Street, P.O. Box 1102
Fairfield, IA 52556-1102
800-624-5893
Updated periodically; $25.
Originally entitled *Book Marketing Opportunities*, this directory lists distributors, wholesalers, sales reps, bookstore chains, book clubs, catalogues, marketing services, mailing list brokers and more. Well worth its price.

Business & Legal Forms for Authors & Self-Publishers
by Tad Crawford
Allworth Press
10 East 23 Street
New York, NY 10010
800-992-7288
1990; $15.95.
Just what the title says. Allworth Press publishes other useful tools for writers too, so you may want to send for a catalogue.

Business Letters for Publishers

by Dan Poynter
Para Publishing
P.O. Box 4232
Santa Barbara, CA 93140-4232
805-968-7277
Updated periodically; softcover $14.95; disk $29.95.
Poynter, the author/publisher of the extremely useful *Self-Publishing Manual* and several other successful books, has compiled a volume of sample letters that includes some to reviewers, ad media, catalogue companies and the like.

The Catalog of Catalogs II: The Complete Mail Order Directory

by Edward L. Palder
Woodbine House
5615 Fishers Lane
Rockville, MD 20852
800-843-7323
1990; $14.95.
Well organized, well indexed information on more than 12,000 catalogues that feature everything from air compressors to yoga equipment.

The Celebrity Phone Book

by Scott Siegel and Barbara Siegel
NAL/Plume
375 Hudson Street
New York, NY 10014
212-366-2000
1990; $9.95.
Direct access to the names, addresses and phone numbers of famous people who may be interested in your work, plus a special section on how to make the most of that all-important first contact.

CMG Mailing List Catalog

CMG Information Services
50 Cross Street
Winchester, MA 01890
617-729-7865
Free.
CMG offers targeted mailing lists of professors who teach specific courses, "decision-maker library lists," and lists of individuals who buy books in a variety of specified subject areas.

CSG Information Services

425 Park Avenue
New York, NY 10022
212-371-9400.
CSG stands for Chain Store Guide. The company's directories may help you zero in on wholesalers and retailers who serve your market.

The Directory of Mail Order Catalogs
Richard Gottlieb, General Editor
Grey House Publishing
Pocket Knife Square
Lakeville, CT 06039
203-435-0868
Updated periodically; $135.
A quick introduction to thousands of companies that sell products of every sort via printed materials. One or more of them might do well with your book.

Directory of Special Libraries and Information Centers
edited by Brigitte T. Darnay
Gale Research Co.
835 Penobscot Building
Detroit, MI 48226
800-877-GALE
Updated periodically.
Information you can use to target information centers, archives and special and research libraries in the U S. and Canada that figure to want your book.

Editor & Publisher International Yearbook
Editor & Publisher Company
11 West 19 Street
New York, NY 10011-4234
212-675-4380
Updated periodically; $70.
This directory of newspapers is a good tool for selling material with a local angle.

Encyclopedia of Associations
Gale Research Co.
835 Penobscot Bldg.
Detroit, MI 48226
800-877-GALE
Updated periodically; $305.
The Encyclopedia of Associations is indispensable. Use the subject index to find groups that care about the topics your book treats. Their members should be interested in buying the book and helping you spread the word about it.

Gale Directory of Publications and Broadcast Media
edited by Donald P. Boyden and John Krol
Gale Research Co.
835 Penobscot Building
Detroit, MI 48226
800-877-GALE
Updated periodically.
With thousands and thousands of entries — arranged geographically and indexed by keywords as well as alphabetically — this is a splendid source of leads to people who might spotlight your work.

Grant Seekers Guide
edited by Jill R. Shellow and Nancy C. Stella
Moyer Bell Limited
Colonial Hill/RFD 1
Mt. Kisco, NY 10549
800-759-4100
Third edition, 1989; $24.95.
"A Rolodex of funders" tells whom to contact about funding and how to handle grant applications.

The Greatest Direct Mail Sales Letters of All Time
by Richard S. Hodgson
Dartnell Corporation
4660 Ravenswood Avenue
Chicago, IL 60640
800-621-5463
Updated periodically; $91.50.
Examples show how leading direct mail copywriters have handled a variety of direct mail assignments.

Guerrilla Marketing:
Secrets for Making Big Profits From Your Small Business
by Jay Conrad Levinson
Houghton Mifflin Co.
One Beacon Street
Boston, MA 02108
800-225-3362
1984; $8.95.
A popular primer on marketing all sorts of things through all sorts of channels, from classifieds to TV, telephone and radio. Levinson's sequel, *Guerrilla Marketing Weapons,* is just out (NAL/Plume, 375 Hudson Street, New York, NY 10014; 212-366-2000; 1990; $9.95).

Guide to American Directories
B. Klein Publications Inc.
P.O. Box 8503
Coral Springs, FL 33065
305-752-1708
Updated periodically; $75.
Arranged by subject and designed to help businesses locate new markets through the mailing lists of national organizations, this directory can lead writers to groups and reference materials relevant to their marketing campaigns.

The Handbook of Nonsexist Writing
by Casey Miller and Kate Swift
HarperCollins
10 East 53 Street
New York, NY 10022
800-242-7737
Second edition, 1988; $5.95.
It is possible — even easy, after a bit of practice — to use nonsexist language without awkwardness or ostentation. This book shows how. Highly recommended. (See also *The Nonsexist Word Finder*.)

How Many Books Do You Sell in Ohio?
by Bill Gordon
818 Via Alhambra, #N
Laguna Hills, CA 92653
818-566-6855
1986; $11.95.
Amusing and frequently enlightening quotes about assorted aspects of the book world.

How to Get Happily Published
by Judith Appelbaum
NAL/Plume
375 Hudson Street
New York, NY 10014
212-366-2000
Third edition, 1988; $9.95.
To find still more strategies and resources for boosting your book's sales, consult the guide that's been called "the most useful tool anyone who writes can buy."

Hudson's Subscription Newsletter Directory
Hudson's
44 West Market Street
PO Box 311
Rhinebeck, NY 12572
914-876-2081
Updated periodically; $99.
Information on newsletters around the world, some of which will be receptive to material from and about your work.

International Directory of Little Magazines & Small Presses
Dustbooks
P.O. Box 100
Paradise, CA 95967
916-877-6110
Updated periodically; $23.95.
The subject and regional indexes in this annotated listing of thousands of small publishing operations can lead you to periodicals that may excerpt, review and/or serve as sensible advertising media for your work. Available from the publisher as well as in your library.

Literary and Library Prizes

edited by Olga S. Weber and Stephen J. Calvert
R. R. Bowker
245 West 17 Street
New York, NY 10011
800-521-8110
Updated periodically; $26.95.
Writers get hundreds of prizes every year in an amazing array of categories. Help your publisher submit your book for the ones that are appropriate for you; winning can boost sales, income and prestige.

See also *Grants and Awards Available to American Writers,* under PEN.

Literary Market Place

R.R. Bowker
245 West 17 Street
New York, NY 10011
800-521-8110
Published annually; $124.95.
LMP is a multipurpose reference work. Familiarize yourself with the directory's major sections, paying particular attention to "Review, Selection & Reference," "Radio & Television," and "Public Relations Services."

Mystery Writers of America

236 West 27 Street
New York, NY 10001
212-255-7005.
MWA publishes the *MWA Mystery Writers Handbook* and *The Third Degree,* an informative source of current news that will interest crime writers.

National Directory of Catalogs

Oxbridge Communications
150 Fifth Avenue, Room 636
New York, NY 10011
212-741-0231
1990; $145.
A wealth of valuable facts about 4,200 U.S. and Canadian catalogues, one or another of which might include your book among its offerings.

National Radio Publicity Outlets and TV & Cable Publicity Outlets

Morgan Rand Publishing Co.
2200 Sansom Street
Philadelphia, PA 19103
800-354-8673
Updated periodically.
Contacts, formats and topics for thousands of radio and TV programs with names and phone numbers.

National Trade and Professional Associations of the United States
Columbia Books Inc.
1212 New York Avenue, N.W.
Washington, DC 20005
202-898-0662
Published annually; $55.
These lists and descriptions of 6,300 organizations, and the indexes to them by product, profession and location, should be useful for finding special sales outlets.

The Nonsexist Word Finder: A Dictionary of Gender-Free Usage
by Rosalie Maggio
Beacon Press
25 Beacon Street
Boston, MA 02108
617-742-2110, ext. 596
1988; $9.95.
Sometimes it's tough to be a nonsexist writer. Here you'll find ways to avoid "businessman," "henpecked," "waitress" and more. This book provides alternatives for roughly 5,000 sexist words and phrases. (See also *The Handbook of Nonsexist Writing.*)

1001 Ways to Market Your Books for Authors & Publishers
by John Kremer
Ad-Lib Publications
51 North Fifth Street
P.O. Box 1102
Fairfield, IA 52556-1102
800-624-5893
1989; $19.95 Hardcover; $14.95 softcover.
Kremer really does cover hundreds of things you and/or your publisher can do to round up readers.

PEN American Center
568 Broadway
New York, NY 10012
212-334-1660.
PEN issues *Grants & Awards Available to American Writers*, a comprehensive, easy-to-use and economical directory, along with a newsletter and other material about issues of interest to writers. The organization also holds parties, runs programs and takes political stands from time to time. Call or write for a free list of publications.

PEN Center USA West
1100 Glendon Avenue, Suite PH
Los Angeles, CA 90024
213-824-2041.
This West Coast branch of PEN, a lively and growing group, works through standing and ad hoc committees to "foster a sense of identity and community among writers in the Western United States" and to advance freedom to write around the world.

Poets & Writers
72 Spring Street
New York, NY 10012
212-226-3586.
You don't have to be a member to get information from Poets and Writers. They publish a magazine replete with useful facts and ideas; *A Directory of American Poets and Fiction Writers,* which can bring you invitations to lecture and do readings if you're listed on it; a list of programs that hire writers to read, lecture and give workshops; and a list of literary bookstores in the U.S., among other things.

Professional's Guide to Public Relations Services
by Richard Weiner
AMACOM
135 West 50 Street
New York, NY 10020
212-586-8100
Updated periodically: $95.
Detailed listings of communications and image consultants, computerized news and broadcast monitering services, media directories, motion picture distributors and a host of other services useful in publicity campaigns appear here.

Public Relations Society of America Information Center
33 Irving Place
New York, NY 10003
212-995-2230.
The country's largest collection of materials about public relations, open to the public for a modest fee from Monday to Friday, 9-4:30. Call ahead to make an appointment.

Publicity for Books and Authors: A Do-It-Yourself Handbook for Small Publishing Firms and Enterprising Authors
by Peggy Glenn
Aames-Allen Publishing Co. Inc.
1106 Main Street
Huntington Beach, CA 92648
714-536-4926
1985; $12.95.
A thoroughly practical handbook replete with solid, specific advice.

Publisher's Lunch
by Ernest Callenbach
Ten Speed Press
P.O. Box 7123
Berkeley, CA 94707
415-845-8414
1989; $7.95.
Get an inside look at the way editors and publishers think by joining an editor and her former flame-turned client as they discuss his new book over the course of six lunches.

Publishers Weekly
249 West 17 Street
New York, NY 10011
800-842-1669
$97 for a one-year subscription.
PW has no equal as a source of up-to-date information about book publishing strategies, trends, people and promotion opportunities. It's available at libraries as well as by subscription.

Research Centers Directory
Gale Research Co.
835 Penobscot Building
Detroit, MI 48226
800-877-GALE
Updated periodically.
Use the subject index to pinpoint research facilities of various kinds that may want to order — and spread the word about — new books in their fields. Roughly 12,000 centers are described.

Rotten Reviews (1986, $12.50)
Rotten Reviews II (1987, $12.95)
Rotten Rejections (1990, $12.50)
Pushcart Press
Box 380
Wainscott, NY 11975
516-324-9300.
If you're a struggling author, you'll find comfort in these negative reactions to works that went on to become classics and/or bestsellers. (Editors even passed up *The Clan of the Cave Bear* by Jean Auel, whose books have now sold more than 20 million copies worldwide.)

Sensible Solutions, Inc.
275 Madison Avenue
Suite 1518
New York, NY 10016
212-687-1761
This consulting firm, run by the authors of *The Writer's Workbook*, helps writers and publishers reach the markets for their books.

Society of Children's Book Writers
P.O. Box 298
Mar Vista Station
Los Angeles, CA 90066.
The society offers a variety of services to people who write, illustrate or are otherwise involved with children's books.

Standard Periodical Directory
Oxbridge Communications, Inc.
150 Fifth Avenue, Room 636
New York, NY 10011
212-741-0231
Updated periodically.
Information about more than 75,000 periodicals in the U.S. and Canada.
Useful for compiling publicity, sub rights and advertising lists.

Standard Rate and Data Service, Inc.
Call 800-323-4588 for a free brochure.
The various SRDS publications provide information about placing ads in
newspapers and magazines and on radio and TV.

Subject Guide to Books in Print
and **Subject Guide to Children's Books in Print**
R.R. Bowker
245 West 17 Street
New York, NY 10011
800-521-8110
Updated periodically.
Excellent tools for assessing the competition and identifying people who
might write blurbs and reviews. Check the listings for forthcoming books too.

Syndicated Columnists
by Richard Weiner
Larimi Communications
1515 Broadway
New York, NY 10036
800-336-3535
Updated periodically; $95.
This book can lead you to individual columnists who figure to like your work
and whose plugs can send sales soaring.

Thomas Register of American Manufacturers
Thomas Publishing Company
One Penn Plaza
New York, NY 10119
212-695-0500
Updated periodically.
A huge compendium listing products and services and carrying advertising,
this can be a fine source of leads to potential premium sales.

Ulrich's International Periodicals Directory
R.R. Bowker
245 West 17 Street
New York, NY 10011
800-521-8110
Updated periodically.
More than 70,000 periodicals from all over the world are listed here.

Women's National Book Association

160 Fifth Avenue
New York, NY 10010
212-675-7804.
This organization is also open to men. Members include librarians, agents, artists, educators, critics and booksellers as well as writers and people in publishing, and they communicate through meetings as well as newsletters.

A Writer's Guide to Copyright

Poets & Writers, Inc.
72 Spring Street
New York, NY 10012
212-226-3586
Second edition, 1990; $6.95.
A clear, concise summary of copyright law accompanied by sample forms and a glossary of unfamiliar terms.

The Writer's Guide to Self-Promotion and Publicity

by Elane Feldman
Writer's Digest Books
1507 Dana Avenue
Cincinnati, OH 45207
513-531-2222
1990; $16.95.
Because it offers such a generous supply of pointers and examples, Elane Feldman's handbook is inspiring as well as enlightening.

The Writer's Lawyer:
Essential Legal Advice For Writers and Editors in All Media

by Ronald L. Goldfarb & Gail E. Ross
Times Books
201 East 50 Street
New York, NY 10022
800-242-7737
1989; $19.95.
Two lawyers who specialize in media and literary law offer a readable, well organized introduction to questions writers often face and "suggest the general answers that should guide them in their work."

The Writer's Legal Companion

by Brad Bunnin and Peter Beren
Addison-Wesley
Route 128
Reading, MA 01867
800-447-2226
1988; $14.95.
Spirited, practical guidance that takes account of developing trends as well as fundamental issues.

Target Marketing Worksheets _____

The worksheets in this kit are designed partly to break tasks down into segments that are easy to handle, partly to help you avoid short-circuiting progress by inadvertently omitting any steps necessary to reach a goal, and partly to provide a record of actions taken.

You're welcome to make additional copies of the forms for your own use.

Blurb Writers and Reviewers

It is never too early to start pinpointing the influential people who can help you by commenting publicly on your book. Make sure you have at least two or three blurbs ready in time to meet the deadline for cover copy. And to improve the odds for success when you approach an individual about providing a blurb or volunteering to do a review, make the rationale behind your approach as specific and personal as you can.

Cover copy deadline is_____.

Reviewer or Blurb Writer _____

Title_____

Address _____

Phone Number _____

Who should contact (you, in-house person, other?)

_____

Rationale (What do you want and why should this person give it to you? Mention connections, credentials, common interests; indicate knowledge of this person's relevant accomplishments)

_____

Nature of request (blurb or review)

_____

Date of request

_____

Form of book sent (ms., galleys, bound book)

_____

Response (date and details)

_____

Is follow-up necessary? If so, when and how?

_____

Blurb (or review) circulated to (names and titles)

Reviews

   Ideally, reviews run on or about publication date, so schedule submissions accordingly, bearing in mind that most periodicals come out earlier than the cover date indicates and that you must allow three to four times the periodical's frequency as a "lead time" (e.g., submit material to a monthly magazine in May to get a piece into the issue dated October, which will really come out in September).

   Again, the more specific and personal your rationale, the better your chances of getting coverage.

   See Resources for directories, and get a lot of reviews in the works; they'll help even if the timing isn't ideal.

Periodical _____

Address _____

Phone Number _____

Issue to aim for

_____
Deadline

_____
Possible reviews (staff or other)

_____
Person to contact (reviewer on staff? someone else?)

_____
Who should contact (you, in-house person, other?)

_____
Rationale (Why will your book be especially interesting and valuable to this reviewer? To the readers who will see this review?)

_____
Approach made (date and other details)

_____
Is follow-up necessary? If so, when and by whom?

_____
Copy sent (date and form of book – ms., galleys, bound book?)

_____
Date of issue with review

_____
Review circulated to (names and titles)

Special Press Release Recipients___

As a matter of course, a press release will go to a long list of media people, most of whom will ignore it. A handwritten, personal P.S. should get selected recipients to pay attention, though, and people involved with smaller, special-interest media are likely to focus at least briefly on a release if they can tell from the headline or a handwritten note that it's relevant to their work.

Deadline for submitting draft press release_____.

Date when finished releases will be available for hand-written addenda_____.

Press Release Recipient _____

Title_____

Address _____

Phone Number _____

Description of periodical, column, show, etc.

_____

Deadline

_____

Angle for handwritten P.S.

_____

Release sent with P.S. (date)

_____

Results

_____

Results circulated to (names and titles)

_____

Follow-up possibilities

Excerpts and Adaptations

Like reviews, excerpts and adaptations of material from your book should run in a variety of periodicals on or about publication date if possible, and the same calculations about the timing of submissions will be necessary. But any exposure at any point will help sell books, and perhaps bring in some extra money in the form of payment from the magazine or newsletter as well.

Periodical _____

Address _____

Phone Number _____

Issue to aim for

_____

Editor to contact

_____

Who should submit (you, in-house person, agent, other?)

_____

Angle of approach and brief description of content (Why this periodical? Why this editor? Why this format and subject matter?)

_____

Query submitted (date)

_____

Response

_____

Manuscript submitted (date)

_____

Response

_____

Results circulated to (names and titles)

Radio and TV

Most books are never discussed on network shows and it's just as well; most books don't have the broad distribution that translates this kind of exposure into sales. Use these sheets to identify *only* those radio and TV shows that are especially appropriate for you and your book, and be prepared to explain your recommendations.

Name and Description of Show _____

_____

Address _____

Phone Number _____

Individual to Contact _____

Who should contact (you, in-house person, other?)

_____

Rationale (Why should this show focus on you and your book? What can you do on the show besides talk?)

_____

Approach made (date and details)

_____

Appearance scheduled (no, or yes and date)

_____

News of booking circulated to (names, titles); be sure to coordinate other publicity, promotion and distribution of copies.

Speaking Dates _____

Since many groups schedule conferences and conventions a year or more in advance, it's smart to start lining up speaking dates early. If you get invited to deliver a talk before copies of your book are available, get names and addresses of people you can send order forms to in due course; and even after you have copies to sell, have order forms handy in case demand exceeds supply.

Meeting the public face-to-face is not only a good way to spread the word about your book; it's a good way to gather reactions and new ideas. And sometimes it's also a way to earn a fair amount of money.

Use the *Encyclopedia of Associations* to supplement your own list of groups you'd like to speak before. And remember that your publisher will probably need to know about speaking dates at least six weeks in advance to get books shipped on time.

Group or Gathering_____

Address _____

Phone Number _____

Individual to contact (name, title, address, phone number)

_____

Who should contact (you, in-house person, other?)

_____

Rationale (What can you offer this group as a speaker?)

_____

Draft letter soliciting an invitation submitted to (name of in-house person and date)

_____

Response

_____

Approach made (date)

_____

Appearance scheduled (no or yes and date, payment provisions and other details)

_____

Coordinated coverage (newspaper, radio and TV possibilities in the area at the time; other possible speaking dates there and then); use additional worksheets as necessary

_____

Books for sale to be ordered by (name and deadline date)

_____

Books to be shipped to (name, title, address, deadline)

Books ordered (date)	Books shipped (date)	Books received (date)

Other materials needed (order forms, posters, etc.) and arrangements to get them

_____

News of this public appearance circulated to (names and titles) (List on back)

Mail Order

The most important thing to remember about direct mail is that potential customers want to know what's in this for them. In selecting lists and drafting copy, focus on the benefits your book will confer on the reader rather than on the book per se.

Mailings can be expensive, so suggest specific lists only when you're confident that you have an angle powerful enough to get action from the people on them.

List (description, size and price) _____

_____

Source _____

Address _____

Phone Number _____

Angle
_____

Other lists suitable for this angle (check for house lists that may fit)
_____

Other house books to piggyback (check current and backlist catalogues)

_____

Are bulk orders possible?
_____

Rough draft of mailing piece submitted to (name and title of in-house person; date)

_____

Response

_____

Mailing scheduled (no or yes and date, size, selection principle)

_____

Bookstores in relevant areas alerted

_____

Mailing sent (date)
_____

Results

_____

Results circulated to (list names and titles on back)

_____

Additional use of this list

Catalogue Sales

Catalogues are an increasingly popular tool for selling books. See Resources for directories, and pursue as many leads as you can. There's lots to gain and virtually nothing to lose. (Catalogues are covered in this Workbook under "Special Sales.")

Catalogue (name, description, size and frequency of mailings) _____

_____

_____

Address _____

Phone Number _____

Kind of copy and illustrations used (get sample if possible)

_____

Deadlines

_____

Terms

_____

Rationale

_____

Who should contact (you, in-house person, other?)

_____

Rough draft of copy submitted to (name of in-house person; date)

_____

Response

_____

Approach made

_____

Book accepted (no or yes and details of mailing schedule, etc.)

_____

Results

_____

Results circulated to (list names and titles on back)

_____

Re-use of this catalogue

Advertising

There's no hard evidence to prove that general advertising does most books much good, so suggest relatively inexpensive ad media that are very closely related to your work and make sure a feedback mechanism is built in to all ads (i.e., include a mail order coupon and an 800 number in each ad or – at the least – information on how to get hold of your book by mail and phone).

Timing of ads should be closely coordinated with publicity, promotion and distribution.

Periodical, Station or Show _____

Address _____

Phone Number _____

Description of audience

_____

Issue or show to aim for

_____

Deadline

_____

Rates

_____

Angle

_____

Other media suitable for this angle (i.e., where can this ad be profitably re-used?)

_____

Coverage to coordinate with (scheduled reviews, publicity, etc.; newspegs)

_____

Draft of ad submitted to (in-house person, date)

_____

Coupon to be used?

_____

Response

_____

Ad(s) scheduled (descriptions, costs and dates)

_____

Results

_____

Results circulated to (list names and titles on back)

_____

Re-use of this medium

_____

Promotional Materials

During public appearances and in nonbookstore retail outlets, an attractive poster and a simple, inexpensive display case can boost sales substantially; everywhere, order forms are a must. Excerpts from blurbs and reviews can be arranged and enlarged to create good posters. Sometimes a blowup of the book cover makes an effective poster by itself.

Description of Promotional Material _____

_____

_____

Uses

_____

Cost

_____

Who will design?

_____

Who will produce?

_____

Request submitted to (in-house person; date)

_____

Response

_____

Material ordered (date, quantity, supplier, delivery date)

_____

Material received (date)

_____

Used for

_____

Results

_____

Results circulated to (names and titles)

_____

Reorders (dates, quantities, etc.)

Especially Interested Bookstores

Bookstore owners and managers who are enthusiastic about your book can help it enormously, so concentrate on them and, at least in the beginning, forget about stores with no special reason to be interested in your work. Especially interested booksellers may be found where your book takes place, where you shop, where your friends have relationships, where books like yours have done well, where the kind of reader you have in mind frequently shops. When you can cite sales results in selected stores they'll help you make headway with other booksellers who have something in common with your early supporters.

Bookstore _____

Address _____

Phone Number _____

Description

_____
Individual to contact

_____
Who should contact (you, in-house person, other?)

_____
Rep for this store (name, address, phone number, schedule of visits)

_____
Rationale (Why should this bookstore be especially interested in your book? Why will its customers be especially ready to buy it?)

_____
Copies ordered so far (note date)

_____
Promo possibilities (parties, readings, posters, other displays)

_____
Promo plans submitted to (in-house person or rep and date)

_____
Response

_____
Promo arranged (description and dates)

_____
Results

_____
Results circulated to (list names and titles on back)

NonBookstore Wholesalers and Retailers

These distribution outlets fit into the so-called "Special Sales" area, but using them is coming to be the norm. Whoever does the contact work may want to wait until finished books are ready (consult your production schedule for the date).

Your editor will know or be able to find out whether the house has already used special sales outlets that should be able to sell your book. Be sure to take advantage of these established relationships if they exist.

Also, whenever possible, work through retailers only to establish a track record of sales in a particular kind of store; then switch your attention to lining up wholesalers who can distribute your book to many stores.

Wholesaler or Retailer _____

Address _____

Phone Number _____

Description

_____

Individual to contact

_____

Has your publisher worked with this wholesaler or retailer before? If yes, when, how and with what results?

_____

Who should contact (you, in-house person, other?)

_____

Rationale

_____

Other books handled by this wholesaler or retailer (list titles and publishers; get sales figures if possible)

_____

Other house books this wholesaler or retailer might handle

_____

Terms

_____

Proposal sumbitted to (name of in-house person; date)

_____

Response

(continued)

Approach made (date and description)

Deal made (date and terms)

Rep who will service this account

Is follow-up necessary? If so, when and by whom?

Sales figures for this account with this book

Re-use of this wholesaler or retailer

Planning Guide and Strategic Calendar

Manuscripts may arrive at a publisher's office anywhere from six months to two years before publication in the normal course of events. On the average, nine months elapse between delivery of a book manuscript and the book's publication date.

A long lead time before pub date can be advantageous if you and your publisher use it to prime the pumps that raise readers' interest levels, by getting advance reading copies out to key booksellers and reviewers or placing short, tantalizing sections of your book with monthly magazines, for example.

If you have any strong feelings about when your book should be published, talk with your editor about them as soon as possible, suggesting, say, a fall date for a book on college sports or a spring date for a book on the concept of rebirth. Then, if the publisher's plans don't jibe with what makes sense to you, discuss the pros and cons of various pub dates. In-house considerations (What else is scheduled for release in the next year?) may be relevant.

Before using the Workbook's Planning Guide and Strategic Calendar, you'll need to coordinate your publisher's production schedule for your book with your own calendar. For instance, you'll want to be available to complete the back-and-forth checking and correcting of the edited and copyedited ms. carefully and well and on time; and while you may choose to work on lists of suitable advertising media far in advance of pub date, you won't want to submit suggestions too soon and risk having them mislaid and never acted upon. Timing is crucial in all areas; acting either too early or too late could throw off the most well-wrought plans.

The Guide/Calendar that follows provides a chronological picture of the publishing process at a glance by enumerating the steps that make it up. Designed to show what's been done and what still needs to be done, the chart may serve you best in the coming months if you tack it up near your desk for updating and ready reference.

As you progress, perhaps you'll find it useful to check off the tasks you've completed in the clear boxes and add new reminders to yourself in the blank spaces.

We urge you to fill in the deadline dates marked with a ✓ right away, and we suggest that you keep dated copies of all letters as well as of all other materials you send out that relate to marketing efforts for your book. You'll no doubt need to refer to them as plans begin to take shape.

Most authors who work at reaching readers find that opportunities multiply after publication. When you take new action on behalf of your book and/or follow up on earlier efforts, it might be a good idea to extend the chart.

One last note: You may have a lot of work cut out for you when your book is being published, but so do all the people at your publishing house. A note of thanks from an author is always appreciated.

PLANNING GUIDE

	Manuscript Handed In	**Book in Production**

Editorial

❑ Have lunch with your editor to celebrate and firm up schedule.

❑ Ask editor to begin introducing you to key players.

❑ Compose letter re line editing.

✓ Line editing begins_____

❑ Check and return edited ms.

❑ Submit design suggestions.

✓ Ms. goes to designer_____.

❑ Check sample pages.

✓ Sample pages due_____.

❑ Compose letter re copyediting.

✓ Copyediting begins_____.

❑ Check and return copyedited ms.

✓ Ms. goes to typesetter_____.

Publicity

❑ Fill out author's questionnaire.

❑ Have photo taken for book cover.

✓ Cover photo deadline_____.

❑ Make blurb candidate list.

❑ Make review copy list.

❑ Make speaking dates list.

❑ Draft speaking dates letter.

❑ Mail speaking dates letters.

❑ Send Xeroxed mss. out for early blurbs to use on cover.

❑ Draft cover copy.

✓ Cover copy deadline_____.

❑ Check prize possibilities and possible directory listings.

Sales

❑ Study Workbook and begin filling out worksheets.

❑ Draft catalogue copy.

✓ Catalogue goes to press_____.

❑ Make sales conference package.

✓ Sales conference dates_____

❑ Make book club list.

❑ Check inclusion in relevant house catalogues.

Work on serial sales:

❑ Make publication list and story ideas list; match stories and markets.

❑ Meet with agent and/or sub rights staff re mss. placement.

❑ Submit queries and/or excerpts to periodicals.

TRATEGIC CALENDAR

Publicity & Sales Efforts Under Way	**Pub. Date**	**Book Reaching Readers**

❑ Check and return galleys (captions, illustrations, headings, index OK?).

❑ Check number of bound galleys ordered.

❑ Approve cover design and copy.

✓ Cover goes to press_____.

✓ Bound books ready_____.

❑ Submit new cover copy for second printing, as appropriate.

✓ Second printing scheduled_____.

❑ Send galleys out for blurbs.

❑ Devise angles for radio, TV and newspaper interviews.

❑ Role-play interviews with a friend.

❑ Devise angles for press releases.

❑ Make press release list.

✓ Press release scheduled for_____.

❑ Contact potential reviewers.

❑ Submit announcement card list.

❑ Compile hometown publicity list.

❑ Request mail order brochure.

❑ Plan library promotion.

❑ Celebrate with friends.

❑ Check to make sure reviews and write-ups are being circulated.

❑ Follow up on serial sales.

❑ Find out size of advance sale.

❑ Make list of publications for ads; suggest ad angles.

Work on special sales:

❑ Make special sales outlet list.

❑ Make catalogue list.

❑ Explore tie-in options for premium sales.

❑ Check available mailing lists.

❑ Draft direct mail letter.

❑ Ask for status report if paperback rights are for sale.

> **Continue reporting good news.**
> **Follow up on projects in the works.**